Be YourSelf
BOLDLY

Honoring the
Free Spirit
Within

Elke Siller Macartney

ISBN #0-9649454-0-1

Library of Congress Catalog
Card Number: 95-062029

Published by:

Voyage Publishing
P.O. Box 1386
Anacortes, WA 98221

10 9 8 7 6 5 4 3 2 1
pbk

Be YourSelf BOLDLY

Honoring the Free Spirit Within

Be YourSelf Boldly is dedicated to the One we are.

I especially salute and offer gratitude to those who
were boldly being themselves as they assisted in this
miraculous process. Thank you to: Ann Jackson, my
amazing scribe, mentor, eternal friend; Jim, my
beloved soulmate and pathfinder;
Ryan and Erin, my little awakening masters, for being
so patient; Chara Curtis, my teacher and word coach;
Chris Terrell, for believing in me;
all the friends who have welcomed Be Yourself Boldly,
for your enthusiasm; and to Inge and Walter Siller,
the ones who nurtured "The Dreamer."

To the one who started it all, Bob Branscom, thanks
buddy.

Forward

*The little girl had the making of a
poet in her who, being told to be
sure of her meaning before she
spoke, said: 'How can I know what
I think till I see what I say?'*

Graham Wallas
The Art of Thought

I am a person who has always been able to
perceive life in a way unique on the planet: I see
auras, or energy fields, around all sentient beings. I
have the privilege and the challenge of seeing
through most of the illusions operating in peoples'
lives and, because of this insight, have been yearning
to find the truth of "what's going on here." I often
watch people say one thing with their mouths while
an entirely different story unfolds in their auras.

I have harbored a vague feeling that I have
forgotten something since arriving on this planet,
and my search for whatever it was that I forgot has
taken me into some colorful and interesting
investigations.

Ten years ago a person entered my life whom I immediately recognized as a kindred spirit. Bob Branscom, a managerial consultant, was freshly arrived from Chicago and ready to begin a new business venture—one based on spiritual principles. He listened to a gentle voice in his head, the voice of Spirit. The voice was clear and spoke with non-judgmental, loving words. I found I recognized something very familiar in the communications that came through Bob.

The three of us, including Spirit, decided to co-create a home study course that would put Spirit into action in peoples' everyday lives. I named it "Be YourSelf Boldly" in recognition of the boldness it would take to come out of the spiritual closet and share what we knew as truth. The creation of this course was incredible: Bob would sit at a computer, his fingers flying over the keyboard as Spirit spoke through him. I asked occasional questions of Spirit, and the answers brought a focus to the flow. I truly admired the ease of this creative process.

Bob and I, in our relationships and in our careers, worked very hard to put into practice the wonderful tenets of "Be YourSelf Boldy." Sometimes we even succeeded. Then there were times when we both slipped into our respective illusions and lived as creatures of habit. But since my introduction to being mySelf boldly, my life has increasingly become a more light-filled, more aware adventure.

After a few years the BYB course fell by the wayside, and I suggested to Bob that it might have a better chance of being practiced by more people were it communicated in the form of a book. That was several years ago. The idea for a "Be YourSelf Boldly" book was put into storage.

In September of 1994 Bob Branscom became fully Spirit again when he died of AIDS. I had the privilege of spending time with him before he released his body, and I was moved by what I experienced with him in his final days. Though his verbal communications became increasingly incoherent, his magnificent Being shone through more strongly than ever. I again brought up the possibility of writing a the book and asked his permission to do so. He gave his blessing with one qualification: "Make it your own, Elke."

My intention to make it my own stayed with me as I tried to find the time to write in my busy life as wife, mother of two boys, inspirational speaker and counselor. In all my trying to make time for the writing, nothing seemed to be happening. Then a miracle occurred.

Another kindred spirit came into my life and suggested I approach writing the book utilizing what made me successful in my work: inspiration. Some of the following messages came to me as I spoke to my friend Ann. Between inspirations, Ann and I would pull weeds, talk, watch Peter Sellers movies, or dance. Each inspirational message came out of my mouth slowly so that Ann could faithfully write down what was being said. I usually tend to lose my train of thought when speaking this way, but since this was Spirit-guided, the words just flowed. I did not necessarily hear a voice in my head (as Bob had), yet each message carried the syntax of a certain personality.

My hope is that you feel the love of all Spirit in these lessons of remembrance. My fondest wish is for you to be reminded of your inspired gift to the world: the gift of being wholly yourSelf.

Introduction to a New Way of Being

*In the faces of men and women I see God, and
in my own face in the glass,
I find letters from God dropt in the street, and
every one is sign'd by God's name . . .*

Walt Whitman
Song of Myself

**An invitation from your Self:
Your presence is requested in a coming out party,
the likes of which you have never seen!**

For many centuries we humans have been operating from a limited world view. Our perception of life has had us thinking that we are humans being born, doing activities, believing in certain cultural rules, living life a certain way, and then dying. We have been participating in our world with only a fraction of our potential, because we have not fully utilized a very important part of our individual and collective lives: the Being. We have acted as if we are simply human doings rather than human Beings.

A lot of us have the notion that we are separate from God, acting alone unless there is an occasional communiqué from "On High." That is the nature of humanity's Fall from Grace. Our Fall was a falling asleep and forgetting that we are actually divine creations of God.

Once upon a time, as you may or may not remember, there were Beings of Light preparing to participate in a grand experiment. These Beings were excited and curious about being a part of a divine plan called "Spirit Residing in Matter." Billions of years led up to this point in creation's manifestations. A particularly beautiful planet awaited seeding of her body with life forms that would also act as her guardians and playmates.

As Beings of Light, we knew we were connected— to God, to the universe, to each other, to the other life forms on the planet. But as the plan unfolded, the allure of becoming material was so great that our gradual descent began. *We started to forget.*

Humans have been very active on the planet for some time now with a combination of wonderful and disastrous results. And what of our Beings? Well, we have always been at play and at work within the human form. We have continually pointed to our common spiritual heritage, sometimes through special teachers, sometimes through our own thoughts and dreams. "You are spiritual creations," our Beings whisper. But for too long we have forgotten our roots.

A new way of Being on the planet has been heralded by many spiritual traditions. Remembering your Self is a huge part of the Grand Plan for remembering who we all are. Participating fully in our individual lives, as both human and Being, will usher in a new dawn of responsibility and stewardship as a planetary group.

The following lessons are an invitation from Spirit to "wake up!" *Be YourSelf Boldly* is not a training program in assertiveness or self-image. It is a commitment to make friends with your own Being, your eternal wellspring of wisdom and love. Your Being is all too happy to participate in your life. Have your human hold hands with your Being; the journey home is so much more pleasant when you are walking with a friend.

Consider this little book as a reminder from your friend, your soul. This is an invitation to play, full out! *Andiamo!* Let's go!

The Purpose of Life

*Very early I knew that the only object in
life was to grow.*

Margaret Fuller Osoli
Memoirs

What is the purpose of life?

The purpose of Life is to be. The purpose of all
that lives is to exist. In that existence, each individual
life brings into harmony, cohesion, and balance the
interaction between matter and Spirit. The dance of
matter and Spirit creates life as we know it—and as
we don't know it, but are soon to discover.

Our discovery will illuminate a unity of Spirit and
matter that has not been experienced in the course of
humanity's existence. Matter has had its heyday for
quite awhile now. Spirit has been relegated to an idea
stored in the attic of the human mind—a concept we
take out, dust off, and examine once in awhile. Yet
Spirit knows itSelf to be more than a concept and is
eager to participate. The dance between Spirit and
matter is in full swing.

Our idea of Spirit changes as we draw Spirit into our everyday lives. We live for those moments when matter and Spirit are in absolute balance (what those who look forward to a "New Age" are actually anticipating). Of course, we don't have to look to the future to witness a new age, it unfolds every day.

The so-called New Age is nothing more and nothing less than the dance of matter and Spirit, stepping together with balance, equality, and mutual respect. The purpose of a human life is to dance towards that goal. We have learned the tango, now we learn the waltz. Our Being has learned to be human, now our human steps into Being. We learn to be a child, an adult. We learn our various roles. All of these dances culminate in the ultimate dance of matter and Spirit—LIFE!

The human purpose is to experience the unity of individual nature with individual body. Be in your body. Let Spirit experience matter moving through time and space. Spirit wishes to see through those eyes of yours, hear through your ears, speak with your tongue, breathe in the air you are breathing, and experience itSelf with a body.

The body lets you know precisely where you are needing attention. It communicates your need to be nourished by affection, acknowledgment, information, food, etc.

The body informs you of your progress in the process of spiritual awakening and evolution. Every breath you take, every dance step you make, everything you perceive, and every feeling of love you have is diligently recorded by your body. Pay attention. It is a marvelous diary or database that can tell you—with very little prompting—what your experiences have been, where they have taken you so far, and where you might go.

The purpose of our human life is to experience it all, which means to live and savor every moment. Know that stepping up to the buffet table of the universe requires your body's participation.

Exercise

In order to fully acknowledge the primary role your body has in your life, choose a day a week that will be Body Appreciation Day. On that day, select one body part on which you would like to focus. Several times during that day, make a mental note of the important functions it plays in your life and what activities it enables you to engage in. Notice its feelings or sensations. Thank it for its important gift to your life.

Example: Your navel, that sweet button of the belly, is the honored part. Important functions, activities, gifts: It holds your belly together. It is an absolute necessity for belly dancing. It is what is left of your original source of nourishing this body into form (the umbilical cord). It bears the gift of your link to humanity; everyone has one. Thank you, dear belly button!

And thank you dear body.

Awareness Through Observation

Few men have imagination enough for the truth of reality.

Johann Wolfgang Von Goethe

Imagine that you are living in a box called **Reality**, your personal reality.

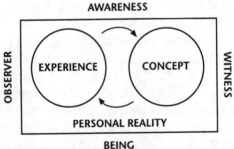

In the box are two domains of existence that interact with each other constantly. It is from within these two domains, called "experience" and "concept," you most frequently view life and plan for future experience.

When you are born you have your first experience in this world; it may be a beautiful experience or it may be pain-filled. Yet it is an experience out of which you form your first concept, or idea. As you go through life you have more experiences, and from those experiences you create more concepts. For example: Perhaps you are born into a family that considers spanking an appropriate action for what is considered a transgression. Out of those experiences of being spanked when you are "bad" you may form some concepts that look like the following: "I'd better keep quiet and be good or I will get hurt." "You can spank me, but I won't show you that I'm feeling hurt. That puts me in charge." "Spanking is bad (or good) for children. When I'm a parent I won't (or will) do that." It is from experience that we form the windows through which we perceive what life is all about.

Another example of basing present day reality on past experiences: I was driving along a busy four-lane road in Seattle. Traveling next to me—for at least a mile—was a policeman who gazed at me intensely. When I noticed this person was giving me a lot of attention, my mind said, "This kind of attention means I'm in trouble." My body chimed in with profuse sweat. I began to wonder if I had been going over the speed limit. Had I run through that last stop light? What on earth had I done wrong? Finally, we reached a stoplight. I stopped. He stopped. I looked over at him nervously. He made a circling motion with his hand. I wondered, "Now what does that mean?" I was still operating from the premise of having done something wrong. Then I realized he wanted me to roll my window down.

"Yes, Officer?"

"That's a great bumper sticker you have there," he said with a grin. "Where did you get it?"

All my experiences with policemen did not serve me in the recent agonizing moments. Nothing in my past prepared me for this new moment.

You might be wondering by now what the bumper sticker said. PEACE BEGINS WITH ME. Yes.

Creating concepts from past experience is the way we learn in this existence called life. Learning and creating beliefs out of past experiences can, for the most part, be useful. But what happens when you want to create something new—a new job, a new relationship, a new behavior? What if this creation does not fit in with any of your previous experiences, yet it is what you want? You'll need to tap into something larger than you've ever known.

How does true creation happen?

Another domain exists outside the box of reality. It is the state of awareness, and it is occupied by the Being, also known as the Observer, or the Witness.

Awareness is the realm of infinite possibility. Outside the box of your limited perceptions, awareness is unbounded and unrestricted. It is from the field of awareness that artists, visionaries, and the effective leaders of this world operate. When you are intent on actually creating what you want, it is from this domain that your personal artist, visionary, and leader make free choices.

The concept/experience box is where every thought is monitored and judged by your beliefs. From those judgments come measured responses in your body and emotions. Those responses create more beliefs that feed your limited world view. As a human, this is not a bad way to live most of the time, but know this: your life will be limited to whatever boundaries you have created. The lines of your box of reality may be long or short, and though these boundaries are artificial walls, they will be experienced by you as real.

A *learned* response comes from the limited judgments of the human. The human has feelings, makes decisions, has physical input and output. The human learns through experience what to judge, who to love and accept, when certain attitudes are appropriate, and so on. The human part of the human Being operates within the confines of time and space.

A *knowing* response comes from the unlimited field of the Being. The Being is not bounded by time or space. The Being of you is eternal.

When you are living your life to the fullest, an intimate dance takes place between human and Being—the former diving into your personal reality box, the latter transcending the box to choose anew. You cannot only live from Being. If you did, you would not experience life as you know it in a body. You would be pure Spirit. Yet here you are in a body, experiencing what you are experiencing, learning what you are learning. What a great adventure! I only recommend that—when you truly wish to create— you create from Being.

The Being always knows the next step and most appropriate choice, because the Being is forever wanting what is most nurturing for your Self. So dance the dance of the human Being and know the power of being Spirit in action.

Intuition

*It is only with the heart that one
can see rightly; what is essential is
invisible to the eye.*

Antoine de Saint-Exupery
The Little Prince

What is intuition?

Intuition is the extrasensory perception of the
Being. The Being receives and communicates information through its intuitive faculties.

In the realm of the human, you have eyes to see,
ears with which to listen, nerve endings to feel
sensations, a nose to smell, and so on. These sensing
devices receive information. Your human communication devices include a voice with which to speak
and sing, hands with which to communicate via
touch or creating things, a body (with a language all
its own), and eyes that signal to others.

In the realm of the Being there are also tools for
receiving information: the inner eye, the inner ear,
the inner feelings. There are ways of communicating

via the inner voice, the inner vision, the inner heart. These inner senses are a part of your intuition which can, literally, see "into-it."

When you follow your intuition's communications, every situation is perceived from a level that reveals undercurrents of truth. For example, someone might say to you, "I am telling you the truth." He may look sincere as he utters these words. You might even think he is sincere, since your experience with him has you believing so. Meanwhile, your intuition is quietly, without judgment, sensing and letting you know this person is not telling the truth. Should you follow your intuition's murmuring you might choose to gently confront that person, or to not communicate with him. The options are myriad, and the choice of how you interact with the information given to you via your intuition is always up to you.

One of the ways to tell the difference between your mind's chattering and your intuition's input is to ask the following question: "Did this communication have any judgment attached to it?" If the answer is no, your intuition is speaking.

Your mind communicates from judgments which are based on your concepts which are based on your experiences. The mind's judgments, therefore, are based on the past. It also extrapolates into the future using the past as the reference. The intuition always communicates in the present moment using present tense, present senses, present information. The intuition never presents its communications with any judgments. The Being has no judgments. The Being's ears, eyes, and mouth neither perceive nor issue judgments.

How can you best operate from your intuition? Is it practical to do so? Let's answer the latter question first. Operating from intuition is eminently practical because it offers the freedom of not having to explain or judge anything. Life is simple and directed when you are in the flow of intuition.

How do you practice being intuitive? You practice by *paying attention*. This is the practice and the game called awareness. In the game of intuitive awareness you consistently step out of circumstance and step into observation. The key word here is consistency. I realize that your training in the box has not made much room for utilizing your intuition. I also realize, however, that you have the ability to act from the place called intuition. In order to break the habit of judging and classifying every input (name calling), practice stepping out of the box and into your greater awareness. I would like to suggest a specific exercise to practice.

Exercise

As you read these words, take a look at one of your hands . . . . As you gaze at that hand, visualize that within the palm of the hand there are two eyes . . . . Now sense that these eyes in the palm of your hand are looking at you, observing you sitting there reading, thinking . . . . Perhaps you have a bemused look on your face as you wonder what's next . . . . As they observe you, the eyes are simply witnessing . . . . Now take that hand and raise it above your head so that the Observer's eyes are peering at you . . . . When you have a clear sense of observing from a place slightly above you, put your hand down but keep the eyes of awareness in place above you . . . . In this way you may practice being Awareness itself.

When you are faced with decisions in your busy life, practice stepping out of the box and into Awareness. You are now being intuitive.

Intuition is the eyes, ears, mouth, and hands of the Being and is forever vigilant. Stepping into observation is always a choice you have as a human Being. As with any other practice, the practice of using your intuition will see you through to mastery. You are already an intuitive prodigy. Uncover this hidden talent and listen to your life's song.

Your Inner Teachers

And sometimes, when our hearts grow faint
Amid temptations fierce and deep,
Or when the wildly raging waves
Of grief and passion sweep,

We feel upon our fevered brow
Their gentle touch, their breath of balm;
Their arms enfold, and our hearts
Grow comforted and calm.

J. L. McCreery
There is No Death

Who are your inner teachers and how do you contact them?

Your inner teachers are Beings who have agreed to assist in your process of evolution and education. They are dear souls who either have or have not been in bodily form at one time or another. The types of inner teachers vary to a great degree, because all are uniquely attuned to facets of your Being. These inner teachers can be seen both as guides on your path and

as colleagues, or spirit mates, who help alleviate the
loneliness of your journey.

Before you entered into this particular incarnation you met with your Spirit guidance committee,
which includes your guardian angels and inner
teachers. This committee assists you lifelong. You, in
agreement with the committee, planned some of
your life's lessons and selected the Beings who would
assist in the implementation of this plan.

Why would you want to contact this committee
now? Because the allure of living in a body and being
immersed in matter is quite tricky at times and could
stand some perspective by those who are not harbor-
ing any attachments to form. These formless ones are
objective and can assist your observation process
when you are challenged by life's many opportunities
to evolve and grow.

You can connect with your inner teachers at any
time. The best time is during meditation or prayer
practice, when you have stopped most of the mind's
chatter and are able to listen. This is important, for
your inner teachers do not like to yell.

Inner guides can also be contacted by your
intention to know how you are assisted and by whom.
In other words you can just ask, at any time, to know
your inner teacher. Right now might be a good time
to introduce yourself to one of your teachers:

Exercise

*In your mind's eye, picture a quiet, sacred space in
nature or a quiet place in a room . . . . This is a special
place for you that you have perhaps discovered in other
meditations or maybe this place is newly discovered . . . .
Quietly feel an expectancy in your heart . . . . You are
waiting for a guest . . . . Gaze at a natural entrance to*

your place, be it a door, or a trail, or an opening . . . .
Notice that the entrance is being filled with a presence . .
. . This presence may look like a person or a spirit or an
animal . . . . The form does not matter . . . . Welcome
your inner guide to your sacred space . . . . Whatever
occurs between you will be natural, spontaneous, and
purely your own.

You can obtain an answer from your inner guides
when you are about to make a choice or a decision, or
you can simply feel the presence of your guides and
know that you are unconditionally loved by at least
one other being in the universe.

Inner guides are particularly trained for their
posts, especially those who are known to you as the
guardian angels. Your angels are committed to your
evolutionary process and are guarding you from two
things:

1. They are here to guard you against any un-
timely departure from your body. You are here to
complete a certain mission. The guardians will make
sure you are able to complete and attend to whatever
you need to learn while in this incarnation. In other
words, they can keep you out of harm's way. When
you are feeling especially fearful, you may want to ask
for their direct assistance. You may wish to call on
your guardian angels at the beginning of your day,
before you undertake a new journey, or after you've
survived a narrow escape to thank them for their
protection.

2. Guardian angels guard against your forgetting
completely who you are. The veil of forgetfulness is
lowered over just about every human Being, but
sooner or later, the veil will start to lift. Those hands
that assist in this lifting belong to your personal

guardian angels. In order to aid your remembrance, they may toss all sorts of hints your way as to who you really are. The hints may come in the form of other people or through such varying forms as TV programs, books, billboards, or a sunrise. As you wake up, you will more and more recognize the designs and reminders of your awesome spiritual heritage.

Other types of inner teachers can include friends, parents, or siblings—whether from this lifetime or ones past. Some guides have been teachers of yours in the past and are returning, with your agreement, to that task. They are especially tuned-in to your life's purpose and are assisting you in a personal way.

Because they are not limited to being in one place at a time, some guides can speak to and through many people. That is why those of you who have attended the phenomenon of channeling are aware that some beings are found to be channeled by more than a few people. These are master teachers who are here to assist in the heralding of a new dawn in human consciousness.

Guidance comes in many forms. I feel the presence of my inner teachers when I am wondering about where this planetary experiment is leading (and certainly my guides are present as they and I explain this process to you). My inner teachings sometimes come in the form of dreams. At other times words float through my head, or I see an eagle soaring just when I am thinking about something that is important to me.

Look to your Self and know Self is intimately connected to not only your three dimensional friends and family, but also to the family of Light that holds you dear on the other side of the veil. Use your inner guides' wisdom to connect again with divine Love, and know that you are constantly in the embrace of your spiritual friends.

Telling the Truth

No pleasure is comparable to the
standing upon the vantage-ground
of truth.

Francis Bacon
Essay on Truth

What is it about telling the truth?

Telling the truth works. It affords two opportunities:

1. The opportunity to clear and release.
2. The opportunity for a new beginning
   and a new creation.

When you tell the truth, you know where you're coming from, where you stand, and where you are going. When you lie to yourself or anyone else, you create a false past, a false present, and, subsequently, an unclear future.

How do you tell the truth in your life?

You tell the truth by allowing it to emerge, unjudged, in every moment. When you look deep within and communicate from your Being, you cannot help but tell the truth.

Within the box of your reality, it is not so easy for your human to tell the truth. Operating from your temporary circumstances and limited beliefs, you can be seduced into lying because you are operating from illusion. Your Being always knows the truth. Your human is not so sure. It is tempted to cover its tracks, to defend or to hide just in case you lied in the past and just in case it is too dangerous for you to come out and be yourSelf. If you are operating from this illusion (temporary circumstances, limited beliefs), all the spiritual tricks in the world cannot manifest the love, peace, and abundance you desire. Only telling the truth creates what you want.

When next you are facing a choice or decision— be it large or small—check in with your Being. The pebble of truth drops into the pond of infinite creation and creates a ripple effect of harmony and true abundance.

Exercise

Try this today: For one day, whenever you are about to make a choice or decision (such as what brand of yogurt to buy, or should you stay in a relationship or not), ask yourSelf the following question:

"What is the truth here and now?"

*Receive your answer and **act on that answer**. Know that, because of your training and because of the fear of* *making the wrong decision, your human will come up with a million and one considerations after you have answered the question. Hold fast to the truth.*

You have the power to choose freely and to tell the truth. Remember: each time you tell the truth, you let more light into this world. The truth shall set you free. The truth shall set us all free.

Integrity

This above all: to thine own self be true,
And it must follow as the night the day,
Thou canst not then be false to any man.

William Shakespeare
Hamlet

What is integrity?

Integrity is a lifelong program devoted to the integration of Self into your life's activities. Integrity is a result of your inner wisdom guiding your outer presentation.

When you are in integrity you operate in the world as a Being who takes stands. "Taking a stand" means to stand in the center of your Being and to know all your actions are choices. Every aspect of living your life flows from this command center. Taking a stand from Self and being in integrity in the world are one and the same thing.

You are out of integrity when you allow circumstances and perceptions to rule your life. The need for outside acknowledgment comes from a lack of integrity with your Self.

Gaining self-worth through outside channels is an indulgence in arrogance. It is arrogant to think the outside world offers you more than the infinite realm of Being. It is through this arrogance that we find ourselves having to lie, hide, and generally not be responsible for our lives.

When we choose to listen only to others' input without checking in with Self, we will find the winds of circumstance are able to easily buffet us about. For instance, if my circumstances happen to include money in the bank, food to feed my family and myself, a roof over my head, *and if I credit these circumstances for my sense of well being,* I will live with a certain amount of contentedness and complacency.

Should my circumstances change radically and negatively: an earthquake renders my living space unusable, the house was uninsured, we need to use the money in our savings to rebuild, we eat poorly because of lack of money, *and I depend on my circumstances for my well being,* I will now feel miserable and victimized. I am a victim when I am out of integrity, relegating my happiness to what I see the world dishing out to me.

When I am in integrity, I may be involved in the same circumstances: food to eat, a roof over my head, and money in the bank. I may be grateful for this present creation, *but I do not need these circumstances in my life to feel fulfilled.* My fulfillment comes from living in integrity with Spirit. And when an earthquake comes I receive directions from my Self and create anew.

Being in integrity means never having to say you're sorry for the adventures you've lived, the choices you've made, or the times you've listened to the call of Spirit at the risk of ridicule. It means you're never sorry for making a free choice. Results come from all choices. The results may or may not be pleasant or comfortable. When you are in integrity, you will know the gift is in having made the choice from the center of your Being.

Being in integrity is a program of learning and evolution that requires attention to the subtleties in life. It demands your attention to all input, no matter the source. You process the input through your Self and act from there. The key to living a successful life is in your integrity to your Being.

Know that Spirit always wants the best—first-class, the maximum, the penultimate—for your wonderful life. Integrity is who you are as an integrated human Being. Stand in the center of your wonder and gaze out on the world through the eyes of a master. Be yourSelf boldly and with integrity. When you come from Spirit there are no actions out of order.

The Mind

*The only means of strengthening one's
intellect is to make up one's mind about
nothing—to let the mind be a thorough-
fare for all thoughts. Not a select party.*

John Keats
To George and Georgiana Keats

What is the mind's purpose?

The mind is a tool created to perceive your
circumstances so that you may act on them. By
circumstances I mean those motions and emotions
that surround you and play with you and give you
the expression you call life. The mind is engaged in
the interaction between your circumstances and your
reactions to them. An example of this is the experience of driving in your car and knowing how to react
when you see a rectangular box with a red light
glowing at you. The circumstance is the red light.
Your mind translates the experience and informs your
body to press on the brake and stop the vehicle,
directing your reactions based on its translation of
your present experience. As translator, the mind is a
potent tool.

Residing within your mind is the Kingdom of Beliefs. The kingdom's borders are a wall of concepts built from past experiences. Inhabitants of this kingdom are thoughts created by your mind.

There is a group of thoughts within this kingdom I will call the "what-ifs." The what-ifs believe they see into the future. They like to make predictions. They love new ideas. They are not aware of the fact that their predictions and new ideas are based on past experiences. The what-ifs are a colorful group of thoughts, speaking eloquently of what could happen. But the what-ifs are still looking to the past in order to predict the future.

Once in a while you will see a rebel in this group. This rebel is a restless sort and tires of reveling in the drama of past circumstances, wishing to move on to a new creation. We will call this rebel "I-will." I-will creates out of the realm of Being, experiencing this realm as infinite potential. Being, as I-will sees it, has no boundaries limited by past circumstances or beliefs. I-will is a true visionary who tunes into Spirit often in order to act from Its voice. I-will acts with wings spread to become "I freely choose."

Choice is consistently available to the Being. As human Beings, we often feel that circumstances are dictating our lives. But, low and behold, the interaction between the mind's limitations and the Being's choices clears the space for the dance of matter and Spirit. Victor Frankl, when he found himself in the horrible circumstance of living in a concentration camp during World War II, observed many who chose to express life. They shared of themselves to their last scrap of bread, their last breath. Amidst the horror all around them, they let their Being shine through.

I have personally interviewed dozens of people who are surviving and thriving after the diagnosis of a terminal illness. These people, who have minds just as powerful and just as limited as yours and mine, have one thing in common: they know they have choices. They can choose how to handle their lifestyles, or how they will react and interact with their illnesses. They can freely choose which healing modality best suits their souls. That is why they are living testimonies to the loving potential of Being.

You, in whatever circumstance surrounds you, can freely choose your interaction with that circumstance. Note that interaction is different from reaction. Reaction is based on the past. Reaction means to act again and again and again to similar circumstances based on past experiences. Interaction is a dance you create and enter into. It is a relationship between your experience (or circumstance) and your Spirit (or Being). The Being simply witnesses the circumstance and then freely chooses how to act. Interaction is influenced by inner choice; reaction is influenced by outer circumstance.

What if —after years of meditating, practicing positive thinking, and eating healthy foods—you find yourself in a circumstance called "diagnosis of cancer"? Your mind's reaction to the diagnosis might be, "But I've been doing everything right. Why is this happening to me? I must be doing something wrong." You dig into your past to find the wrong turn, the wrong food you ate, the wrong meditation practice, and the day you were not so positive. After a while you may find this activity of searching for the wrong to be rather fruitless. You might even find yourself becoming more ill.

Your mind then tries another tack. Let's say you were given information from the experts of medical science that certain treatments give certain results based on certain experiences witnessed in the past. Your mind wishes for you to bank on utilizing these proven treatments; however, your Being whispers that you will not respond to these treatments but will respond to something else. A conflict ensues based on what your mind feels *should* be done and the *choices* offered by your Being. Perhaps you disregard the inner messages and try the treatments, even if you don't believe in them. Your mind says, "Past medical experience has shown that this may do some good." For a while you are convinced this will do the trick. You initially feel better, but doubts return to your conflicted mind and you again find yourself facing a deteriorating body.

There may then come a time when you are face-to-face with death itself. At this point the mind can no longer serve you, for death is an experience it cannot grasp and greatly fears. Yet the Being, knowing itself to be eternal, consistently and graciously offers you free choice. You may choose to continue in this existence called life or you may choose to discontinue. Your options are unlimited.

The Being is who you are. This experiment called "Matter and Spirit Cohabiting" is a lot more fun when you open your mind to the choices of Spirit.

Ego

Every man is of importance to himself.

Samuel Johnson

What is the ego and what is its purpose?

Within the Box of Personal Reality, the ego is both general contractor and maintenance operator, calling the shots on how the box will be built and maintained. Its function is to create walls and boundaries for the survival of your individual. It appears as the limited self within the unlimited Self.

Like a muscle in the body, ego grows strong when exercised and diminishes (even atrophies) when not. When ego feels strong, secure, and confident in its usefulness, it expands to a level of life enhancement. When ego is feeling useless and neglected, it contracts to a level of defensiveness—its very survival is threatened. The limits of ego change with changes in consciousness.

Here are some needs of the ego and examples of how contracted and expanded egos operate differently when trying to meet these needs:

1. *Social structure and status* guarantee a place for the individual. You feel secure when you know your individual place in the world because you know who you are and how to act. Ego loves clubs. Differences and pride in cultural groups are heaven for the ego who thrives on identity. If you belong, you are important enough to be cared for.

When the ego is expansive, a sense of community is achieved. Creating community has been an essential pathway to growth for humanity. Within a community, members learn to communicate, to live in peace, to grow and learn together. Moral character can only be developed within a community structure, and ego is all too happy to hold an individual to laws of conduct.

When ego is contracted, separation is emphasized. A sense of community can change to a feeling of paranoia about the "other." Rules and laws constructed by contracted ego are used to promote control, rather than to promote peace. Hatred breeds in an atmosphere of distrust. Personal and group skirmishes occur. The contracted ego does not help to open the lines to communication, rather it fans the flames of righteousness and separation.

2. *Active participation* in life gives ego the security of knowing you are interested in being alive. If you are busily involved in life-supporting activities—gathering food, ensuring shelter, creating work situations, creating relationships, creating drama—you will feel a sense of accomplishment. To the ego, accomplishment ensures your importance, which, in turn, enhances your chances of survival.

The expanded ego feels alive and in the flow. It participates fully in the creation of a positive reality. New creations that support the individual and society are encouraged. Ego helps to develop nurturing and supportive standards of living for the human.

The contracted ego is a blame machine. Bitter about feeling forced to participate in a tedious life, it is threatened by everything and everybody. It creates a sense of aliveness by investing in dramatic situations. Greed, envy, and intrigue are some of the results of these investments—and they surely do make a body feel alive!

3. *Boundaries* are created to bring focus to a flow. Known boundaries are supported by ego's love of habits. Habitual behavior can create a sense of homeostasis.

Change makes the contracted ego a little nervous. In its need to rest in the known, this ego will practice a behavior over and over and over—regardless of the impact on the human's life. For example: Your ego might like your habit of achieving up to only a certain comfortable success point. When faced with the possibility of succeeding above and beyond your typical comfort zone, ego will use sabotage. Known limits reassure your ego of its control.

When the expanded ego is consulted and assured of its place in future enterprise, it relaxes and allows for new situations to unfold. If a habit is inhibiting the good of the individual, reassessment can take place and changes achieved.

How do you attend to ego's needs while you awaken to your full presence? How might you assure ego of its survival while you rise in consciousness and awareness?

Your challenge is not to try to eliminate ego. If you have a body, you need an ego to work with.

Consider that you are in a relationship with ego. Allow ego to express. Ego assumes it is there for your survival and well being, so it must have its say.

If ego is constantly tripping up your progress and results, you might need to have a conference. You might say:

"Ego, thank you for expressing your concerns. I am honored that you are here to ensure my individuality and my survival as a human. As I ponder which next steps are most appropriate for this Soul, I ask that you please be as vigilant as ever. Express yourself at any time. Know I will sometimes act in ways that might seem scary or threatening to you. I will hear your concerns so that together we may create a harmonious course. I love you. You are important and you will be heard."

Your ego is not in charge of your life, your Self is. However, your Self, as the king or queen of your personal dominion, is allowed to have advisors. Ego is a fine advisor. You may not always heed the counsel of your royal advisor, but you are wise to pay attention to ego's suggestions. Do not deride your ego. If you wish to create beyond ego's advice and needs, that is your choice. But allow ego its chance to be a part of the awakening process.

The Emotional Garden

*There is no fear in love; but perfect love
casteth out fear.*

The Bible

What are emotions for?

Emotions and feeling are wellness indicators of
your body, mind, and spirit. You might consider
emotions akin to the flowers of a given terrain. Upon
close examination, flowers can tell you whether that
area receives great quantities of water or very little,
whether the sun shines on that patch of earth or if it
is under a canopy of trees, if the soil has an abundance of nutrients or if it is sterile, and whether the
climate is hot or cold.

Emotions serve similar functions for the land-
scape of your body, mind, and soul. They are indicators of shifts in your personal climate. It is through
tending your emotional garden that you know
whether you are being nurtured enough, paid attention to enough, and whether you are listening closely
enough to your inner guidance.

How do we use emotions in everyday life?

Many cultural traditions and religious thoughts
relegate emotion to something that needs to be
controlled. Emotions do not need to be controlled;
they need to be felt and paid attention to. If you pay
attention to your feelings—even when they seem to
be out of control—the emotions will quickly subside,
allowing the true learning to come forth. It is when
you repress those feelings that they will shout to be
felt in a stronger way. Repression of emotions can
diminish your sensitivity to what your soul, body,
and mind need to feel alive, present, and well.

Repression of emotions is understandable, since
many people have noticed that some of the more
negative emotions seem to get people and whole
societies in trouble. I would like to suggest that these
troubles begin with the repression of, and the lack of
safe outlets for, emotional outcries. If you provide a
safe outlet for emotions, they will express until they
have felt heard; then they will subside. This is when
the Being, through observation, can assist in deter-
mining the source of the emotions, uncovering why
they were brought up in the first place.

For every emotion there is a cause, as for every
flower a seed. For every experienced feeling there is a
perceived reason to feel that way.

The causes of many of the darker emotions center
around a very basic feeling: fear. Fear is a tremendous
force in a human's life. It is the foundation for such
emotions as anger, grief, sadness, disgust, and envy.
It often seems that this feeling should not be un-
leashed, or that it would be better (safer) if put into a
controlled space. Yet fear does have its purpose. It can
compel people to act and act quickly in the face of
impending danger.

Perhaps that was the original intention for the creation of fear. As a physical response to physical danger, fear was to act as an alarm to alert and prepare the body in perilous situations. Somehow fear has infiltrated your other nonphysical bodies as well. Now your mind can have fearful thoughts (especially of the future based on past experiences), your emotional body naturally feels fear, and your body has a fear response known as fight or flight.

Some situations may not warrant a fear response from your mental or emotional bodies, only a physical response to potential physical harm. Rather than trying to eradicate fear from your nonphysical selves, however, it is perhaps a good time to heal this response, transforming it into a useful lesson. One way of working through fear is to breathe very deeply, right into your belly. This type of breathing is an affirmation to your body, mind, and emotions that you want to live. The shortness of breath that comes along with fear increases the fearful feeling, because it causes the body to think that death or great harm is imminent. Breathing deeply allows your body to relax, which signals that all is well to your mind.

The ultimate transformational agent for fear is love. Love can short-circuit the fear response. The offshoots of love—compassion, understanding, tenderness, centeredness, connection, etc.—help to undermine the feelings of fear. Fear and love cannot exist in the same place at the same time. Anger is a good example of a fear-based feeling that can be transformed by a compassionate touch, a listening ear, an empathetic heart, a human connection.

And what of the other feelings? Feel them and go on about your life. It does you no good whatsoever to shuttle emotions into a compartment to deal with later. You *will* have a later opportunity to deal with those emotions, but by that time the emotions will have built up some steam, making them more un-wieldy to work with. Learn to face and place your attention on these feelings in the moment in which they are felt. This is when they can be addressed and worked with fully. When you pay attention in the now to your feelings, you can also determine the underlying lesson. There are lessons to be learned from every emotional experience.

There are times, especially in today's society, when emotions are difficult to work with because of "appropriateness" issues. As far as your Self is con-cerned, it is always appropriate to feel. Do not place yourself in a position of having to repress your emotions very often, if at all. Soon, very soon, you will have the opportunity to transcend most of the darker emotions. At this time, however, the feelings of sadness, anger, and fear can fuel your passion to act upon some of the present day situations needing attention. At times anger can spur you on to action when neutral feelings or feelings of peacefulness could not. This is not to say you need these emotions in order to act; they are useful tools, barometers of what is happening inside you.

Ask yourSelf often, "How am I feeling about this?" Asking for emotional input and paying atten-tion to the answer gives your Being a chance to assist you. Allow your emotions to speak to you and you will notice that you feel clearer every day. Feel your feelings fully; they need your attention and care. Let your emotional garden grow and blossom. Your personal benefit will benefit all humankind.

Abundance

*All places that the eye of heaven
visits are to a wise man ports and
happy havens.*

William Shakespeare
King Richard II

What is abundance?

Abundance is an outpouring from the inner
vision. An attitude of abundance naturally flows
when you are living a life of vision based on free
choice.

How does vision differ from ideas or pictures?
When you have an idea, it may be a "good" idea or a
"bad" one. The picture of the idea follows the out-
lines of your mind's beliefs. You can add details to the
picture, but that will not change the fact that a
picture is built upon experiences and concepts.

Vision, however, is an inner knowing of the
Being's desire. Your inner vision has no perceived
limitations, only choice. Infinite choce. Base your
actions upon this desire and you will have abundance.

An attitude of abundance puts your desires into manifest form. When you know of your true wealth, your actions will naturally support your vision. Your surrounding circumstances will support you, and the people walking into your life will bring opportunities for meeting your desires.

To illustrate the difference between picturing and visioning: Your Being has a vision called "Becoming a Communicator." Should you follow the song of your Being's desire, your body will naturally react with pleasure to the exciting investigation of becoming a communicator. The mind, loving the tidiness and safety of structure, will want to channel the investigation into a certain form. For instance, the mind might say to your Being, "You should study speech-making for that is the way for you to best become a communicator." The mind's offering is a good one, though limited. Being, seeing an opportunity to communicate, may or may not choose the mind's picture. It sees simply another opportunity. Having checked in with the vision of the Being, you may freely choose which program to follow. That is the gift of tuning in to your vision as well as acknowledging your mind's prompting.

Abundance interacts very well with *both* mind and Spirit. Graceful and rich experiences flow from this interaction. When the mind perceives that you are not experiencing abundance but are experiencing lack, it is time to step out of the box, recall your inner vision (your Being's purpose) and choose again.

A simple exercise to give your mind focus and simultaneously tap into the Spirit's leanings follows:

Exercise

When you are feeling lack, adopt an attitude of gratitude. Survey your surrounding life circumstances and receive the gifts life offers. Often you have heard of people who have lived through difficult experiences (such as AIDS or concentration camps or natural disasters) having acquired the ability to find and acknowledge the gift of their present circumstance. If you perceive what the world presents to you as an opportunity and a gift, you will recall your abundant nature once again.

Abundance is not a program you can necessarily plug into. It is a perception, an attitude. This is not to say that you should not participate in abundance programs and classes, but if you find yourself paying lip service to spiritual principles, you will learn that no program is effective in bringing you the abundance you desire. Come from your heart's desire. Experience life as a fully alive, prosperous Being. Thank Spirit for the gift of life. You are abundantly yourSelf and will always be so.

Being in Relationship

*Friends are not merely one
another's priests or gods, but
ministering angels, exercising in
their part the same function as the
Great Soul does in the whole—of
seeing the perfect through the
imperfect, nay, creating it there.*

Margaret Fuller Ossoli
Memoirs

What is being in relationship?

Relationship is the soul's longing for connection
to itself. When you are in relationship you are con-
necting to another aspect of your Being.

True relationship is inclusive, not exclusive. The
connections made in true relationship always leave
room for more—more involvement, more love, more
connection. True relationship is very roomy indeed,
for it originates from your unlimited Self. True relationship starts with and ultimately ends with your
friendship, love, and respect for Self.

The illusion of a relationship outside of yourSelf
is another construct of the mind. The mind, in its

need for boundaries and definition even has special classifications for different "kinds" of relationships. The mind fosters such categories as intimate relationships versus friendships, familial relationship versus working colleagues, and acquaintances versus true friends. From the mind's perception, these relationships are exclusive of one another. Often we humans tend to think we cannot be friends with our parents or in-laws. Conventional wisdom suggests we cannot be in relationship with someone who doesn't perceive the world as we do, or we should not have an intimate relationship with our boss or coworker. There are many examples of exclusivity in relationship.

True relationship does not see boundary lines. Being in relationship simply means being connected in the moment, Being-to-Being. This principle extends to every relationship in life, for the Being recognizes another Being without the necessity of labeling or defining.

Naturally, since we are both matter and Spirit, choices are open to us. We may choose to marry one human being and work with four other human beings and give birth to two others—and be in true loving relationship with every one of them. Intimacy is always possible from the Being because it regards intimacy as "in-to-me-see." You may see the true me as you allow me to see the true you. In-to-me-see is a call to play. When Beings play together circumstances do not limit the level of intimacy they experience.

Now what of the game called romance?

Romance is a fun game created out of the mind's need to sense the impact of love. The game involves looking to another for exchange of special commodities and gifts that enhance self-esteem, feelings of attractiveness, self-worth, vulnerability, power, and control. These commodities are bartered and traded in the market of the mind, for the mind perceives these things as the needed ingredients for a sense of fulfillment.

In true relationship this market has a limited place. Romance is simply a game, and there is room for many such games in relationship.

Being in love is simply Being. Love is communicated beyond the farthest reaches of any romantic encounter and includes everyone with whom your soul comes into connection. This is not a recommendation against bouquets of flowers and gifts of love. As long as the gifting comes from being Love itself— without regard to bartering, buying, or selling—the love you feel in relationship will always be intensified in the sharing.

Exercise

Today observe the many ways you include others in relationship. As you observe yourSelf including others, give each Being you connect with a gift. The gift may be a smile, a compliment, a hug, an acknowledgment, a gentle touch, a bouquet of flowers and bath salts, or a look straight into a person's eyes. The most powerful way to show your love to another is to listen, pay attention, look directly into the eyes, and to acknowledge him/her from your soul. Loving relationships will take on new dimensions of awareness when you give the greatest gift of all, yourSelf.

Energy Fields

There they stand,
Shining in order like a living hymn
Written in light.

Nathaniel Parker Willis
Poems

What is an energy field?

Your personal energy field, also known as the
aura, is your Being's expression. In the sea of divine
energy known as God, your particular energy field is
an individual wave. Your unique vision and your
unique beingness is God's yearning to create matter
from the infinite variety of God's spiritual essence.

If you'd like, you may consider God to be a
multifaceted diamond, and your aura a ray beaming
off a facet. Each baby is born within that beam of
light. That light is who you are. Do you realize the
profound nature of <u>your</u> nature? To be in a body and
yet be surrounded by an aspect of God, your aura, is a
spiritual truth and a most miraculous creation.

As you operate within the wonderfully unique
light created by Spirit, you are shown your life's

vision. Before you came into this incarnation as a
human, you asked God, "How may I get closer to you
as I create myself in human form?" God's answer was
in the form of a vibration. That vibration—with its
specific tone, color, and feeling—became the You that
you know to be Self.

I see the human Being's energy field as two
simultaneous expressions. One expression changes
from moment-to-moment, reflecting current physical
status, emotions, and thoughts. This is the sentient
human influenced by the limitations of time, space,
and circumstance.

The other expression of the individual aura I see
as the Being. The Being and its unique aura feels no
separation in time or space from anyone or anything.
Your aura's unique resonance and color may tint the
way you perceive the world. (For example, a rose-
colored aura would indicate a highly compassionate
and emotionally empathetic Being.) This aura of
Being reflects the light of your eternal life and will
continue to exist and evolve long after your emotions, physical sensations, and thoughts cease to
exist.

Your eternal Being continually makes choices,
and these, too, are reflected in your energy field. You
are influenced by the agreements made between your
Self and God, yet all agreements are based on free
choice. Even within the parameters you agreed to for
this lifetime (culture you were born into, racial
category, choice of parents, etc.), choice avails you
with possibilities for change and growth. This freedom of choice gives you opportunities to play many
roles in one lifetime. In my lifetime I have played the
role of daughter, wife, lover, friend, salesperson,
dancer, counselor, teacher, student and so on—

probably into the hundreds of roles. Each role you play adds depth, breadth, and variety to the colors in your Being's energy field.

By the way, the existence of energy fields is not confined to just human Beings. There are sentient Beings in this universe of many varieties and creative expressions. Birds have auras, rocks have auras, trees have auras. There is an energy field around that bouquet of flowers you received for your birthday. The Earth expresses herself not only as matter but as energy as well, and I thrill to see her brilliant blue-green aura at times.

We are energy. When you realize your energy connection to all beings in your life, you will no longer hunger or thirst for love. Albert Einstein once said, "I want to know God's thoughts. The rest are details." Your unique expression as an energy field is a thought of God's.

Miracles

*A man is too apt to forget that he
cannot have everything. A choice is
all that is left him.*

H. Mathews
Diary of an Invalid

What is a miracle?

A miracle occurs when you acknowledge you are
a divine creation of God, worthy of the utmost
respect, the clearest love, and all the treasures the
universe has to offer. At times miracles occur when
we *believe* they will occur. Belief is a powerful force in
a human's life. But what of the miracles that are *not
based on belief*? What are these seemingly veiled, yet
very welcome, guests?

Miracles happen every day, even when there is no
faith, belief, or hope involved. Example: An acquain-
tance of mine was diagnosed with an incurable
degenerative disease. A rising star in her profession,
she had thought she "had it all" before becoming ill.
Her disease, she was told, had no cure and ended in a
painful death. At first she did not want to accept the
possibility of dying, so she tried with all her might

and with all her faith to fight this perceived ending. She involved herself in many spiritual endeavors, including increasing her faith in God and utilizing positive thinking techniques. At last, in a wheelchair, hardly able to move more than her head and arm, she knew she was dying. In that moment came a recognition that all her efforts had come to naught. She was going to die.

My friend recognized that, regardless of whether she was going to live or die, she was a child of God. She was a Spirit eternal. Alive and very well today, her miracle occurred in her acceptance of *what is so*. The futility of her mind's struggle brought her to a choice point—and the choice was not between living or dying. The choice was to reckon with the past.

This woman had contracted polio as a child, which rendered her body slightly more crooked than the average body. Nearly all her life she had been in denial of the fact that she actually hated her body; she felt it made her unworthy of love. At the moment of her miracle she reclaimed the unconditional love of Spirit. Her hatred was released. She chose to love herself as is. *Miracles occur when we love what is.*

When you are living your life in integrity with your Self, you know you are responsible for your life. Being responsible means being able to respond with boldness to all situations. Miracles are created when you accept that responsibility and make your life your own.

Your ability to respond (and create a miracle) does not depend upon what or in whom you believe. The mind uses belief as a tool to prop itself up, to prove worthiness. Remember, belief in someone or something is limited. Beliefs are based on information and experiences outside of your Self. Beliefs are usually based on occurrences in the past. They require that you not waver in total acceptance of them. When doubt enters in, beliefs become ineffective. When new information and new possibilities come your way that do not fit into your belief structure, you cannot grow any further than your beliefs will allow.

A man was severely injured on his job as a brick-layer. After many years of rehabilitation he was no better off than he was on the day of his injury. He still did not have work, and his self-esteem had plummeted to an all-time low. When asked by his rehabilitation counselor what he wanted to do, he stared blankly and said, "I don't know. No one has ever asked me that before." "Why?" asked his counse-lor. "Because," said the man, "my grandfather was a bricklayer, my father was a bricklayer, and I knew my place in the world. No one ever asked me what I wanted. I just knew I had to be a bricklayer." His belief structure would not permit him to move on and to create anew, and it did not serve him when he was faced with the possibility of actually having a choice.

With the counselor's help, the man was able to move beyond his beliefs to claim what he wanted. He took responsibility for his life and, in so doing, allowed a miracle to occur. He found his Self, a Self he loved, and took a new job compatible with Self. His life now sings a new song.

There are probably some thoughts running through your mind right now about what you have just read: "I've got to believe in something don't I?" "Only my believing in Jesus (or God, or Krishna, or my Guru, or my doctor) can give me the strength to carry on in my life." "Who am I without my beliefs?"

Who you are is responsibility itself. You are coming from Spirit. You are coming from an unlimited energy source. You are able to respond clearly in your life to whatever situation you find yourself in. The power of living your life to the fullest resides within you.

You may believe whatever you like in any moment. At times beliefs can be helpful. But know that on the eve of tomorrow's promise, beliefs are still singing yesterday's songs. When Copernicus had the audacity and courage to suggest a new cosmology (that the earth revolves around the sun, instead of the other way around), the beliefs of the times could not permit the inevitable consequences of such a profoundly radical view. Today we are blocking new miracles in healing and consciousness by the beliefs we hold to be so true.

Miracles occur when beliefs are dropped and Spirit is known. Accept and love who you are and what you hold true today. Tomorrow life may change, you may change, the world may present you with new and strange opportunities for growth. Believe anything you like, but know your beliefs are limited. Whenever a change or situation seems impossible, the solution might be just outside the box.

Love

*No matter where or how far you
wander, the light is only a split
second, a half breath away, it is
never too late to recognize the clear
light.*

The Buddha
Tibetan Book of the Dead

What have we forgotten?

Under the guise of being human, we have forgotten the essential nature of all creation in the universe.
Nature herself is an aspect of this creation, and all
living beings come into form with this one unifying
element: LOVE. Love eternal and wise, Love in its
purest form has been forgotten for many eons. Yet,
though forgotten, it has continued to fuel and nur-
ture our existence. We also have forgotten that this is
so.

You may remember that our fall from grace was a
falling asleep. When we fell under the spell of forgetfulness, the first and most powerful force that we
closed our eyes to was Love. We, for whatever reason,

placed conditions on Love and relegated it to such categories as emotion or sentiment. Essential Love cannot be categorized as an emotion or sentiment or idea. Closer to what Love really is, is a *force* that when experienced in its true form is known as a feeling, a sense, an absolute knowing

It is in divine Love that we were created. The Creative Feminine Love Force together with the Creative Masculine Love Force brought into being all other forces and creations, including humanity. The allowance of this Love Force is absolute. We are even allowed to experience forgetfulness.

On this planet there have been many manifestations of forgetfulness, a profound example of which is the concept of evil. Evil is simply forgetfulness. Forgetting that you are Love itself brings out the polarity, the opposing force of evil. The darker forces that have reeked havoc in this world can be better understood as the forgetful ones, or the forgetful forces. The one who seems to have disremembered the most is that being you know of as Satan. Satan is a forgetful angel. As we, one-by-one, awaken from our slumber, we each promote the remembrance of the Love Force that is guiding us all, including Satan.

Remembering who you are begins with your acknowledgment of the unconditional, unopposed Love of Creator. The Love Force runs through us all. Remember this truth when you are tempted to fall asleep and allow hatred or jealousy or anger to take over your thoughts.

Exercise

In order for you to wake up when you are submitting to the fearful and forgetful forces, simply do and know the following:

Say to yourSelf often, as frequently as you think of it, "I am Love." You might also add, "As I am a loving presence on this planet, I have the right and the responsibility to be directly in charge of all my thoughts, all my activities, all my feelings. The Love Force in me is the creative force. Love allows me to be whole and complete at all times and in all ways."

Should you remember to remember that you are love, you will be rewarded, for the Love Force is merged with your presence. At that point in time and space, you are beyond time and space. You are Love itself, eternal.

Healing

I am larger, better than I thought,
I did not know I held so much goodness.

Walt Whitman
Song of Myself

What is healing and what is the source of healing?

Healing is remembrance. Whether we are healing the physical body, our emotional turmoil, or the mind's misgivings—the true source of our healing comes from awakening to the power of love. The concept of healing cannot be narrowly defined, for healing appears to us and enters our lives in many guises and forms.

Healing is an eternal process of the evolving soul. Your personal evolution is intimately tied to the healing your soul experiences as it resides within human form. Healing, therefore, is not limited to cures or elimination of disease or unrest. Healing is born through willingness to face and embrace whatever you encounter, *including* disease, ill feelings, judgments, and fear.

You may picture the healing process as your bringing to a negotiating table members of a personal healing committee. The members of this committee are aspects of yourself, and who shows up is dependent on the given situation. The committee can include such illustrious members as your feelings, intuition, mind and its judgments (a committee in its own right), ego, fears, hopes, and dreams. With unity of direction, yet with distinct voice, each states its needs. You will know healing has occurred when each member has spoken in truth and is listened to, even applauded.

Should you find yourself in a situation of ill health or ill feelings, you might want to entertain and graciously pay attention to the committee within you. You may wish to engage in a process such as the following:

Exercise

In uneasy situations, ask yourSelf the following:

"What does my Heart have to say about this situation?"
"What does my Mind have to say?"
"What does my Soul have to say?"
"What does my Body have to say?"

After you have received the answers, ask this next question:

"What does my Heart need in this moment?"
"What does my Mind need?"
"What does my Soul need?"
"What does my Body need?"

When you have heard the answers from these selves, you might acknowledge in the following manner:

"I am wholly healed from within and without. I have heard the call of love and embrace all that surrounds me, including that which is not loving. In so doing, I know from the core of my Being that all is well, for all is held in love."

Healing appears to be subtle at times: a quiet smile creeps across your face in a moment when you spontaneously feel unconditional love for someone who has hurt you. Healing can happen in the very last breath of being human, when there is a realization of the oneness of all. Healing can strike at a moment's notice; be prepared for its exuberant company. In your enthusiasm for human life, you can accept healing without qualm.

Healing, wholeness, love, compassion, forgiveness, embracing that which is unembraceable—all these are forever in unity, as we Beings are forever in One.

Peace be with you. Healing is within you.

Death: The Final Frontier

*All that lives must die, passing through
nature to eternity.*

William Shakespeare
Hamlet

What is death? Why are we afraid of it?

Our forgetful nature after humanity's fall from
remembrance has left us with many fears. Death is a
natural process that scares a lot of people. Why?
Consider the following two popular beliefs about
death:

1. Belief in annihilation. Whether you believe
this termination is a sentence imposed in judgment
by Creator, or that it is simply a "fact of life," your
fear is that this lifetime is "it," and after the body's
last breath you will no longer know life or exist in
any form.

2. Belief in an experience beyond this reality, a
life after death, in which the quality of life is based
upon judgment. An enforcer will reward or punish
you for your lifetime behaviors. You may fear you
haven't behaved well enough, or followed certain
(man-made) religious laws, and so will suffer greatly

after death—otherwise known as you-will-go-to-hell-if-you-are-wicked.

Considering the above, no wonder the fear of death is so prevalent!

The possibility of annihilation does exist, but because of the level of commitment from Creator to this wonderful creation called "life of free will," the likelihood of this permanent termination is extremely slim. All creation is allowed to live and evolve. Even those who have forgotten so greatly that they might be termed "evil" are offered remembrance of their commitment to evolve closer to the Source.

There is also truth to the notion of judgment, but this judgment is not as most popular religions portray. If there is any judgment at all of your behavior, it is created by you and your cultural group. The presence of punishment or reward is made possible by you in agreement with others who will do your Soul's bidding.

If your Soul feels that certain consequences are necessary for evolutionary and educational gains, then the concept you know of as karma will come into play. Karma is simply the principle that for every action is a corresponding reaction in the universe and throughout human lifetimes. You have the opportunity to abide by the constructs of karma or you may create a new reality. The new reality can be formed in a moment's time, and your karmic debts can be cancelled with a brief but heartfelt pledge to your integrity. This is known as the grace that is discovered through forgiveness and surrender of Self into the will of Source.

Karma is just another way of monitoring your evolutionary progress. If damaging behavior is a recurring theme for you in your lifetimes, then consequences to which you agreed before you arrived in a new body can be promoted and utilized for the soul's growth and education.

Most of what the religions deem to be sinful behavior are constructs created by the people who put the religions on the map. The beliefs and laws that produced such terms as "sin" and "evil" were meant to support systems that use fear as a way to control human behavior. In the very near future you will remember your innate sense of integrity and goodness as a spiritual Being intimately connected with Creator. But because you have forgotten this, and those who have made the laws have forgotten as well, there has been a distrust of the integrity of humanity.

One-by-one, you are waking up. As part of this remembrance, you will feel no fear about death. Death is merely a transition, and it will be seen as such by your human self. You will recall that part of the process of your falling under the spell of matter included adopting the veils of forgetfulness at your birth. These veils are being lifted and you will have a *stunning* view. You will see the eternal progression of your individual soul along with the billions of other souls who are making their way home.

I would like to propose another way for you to experience the concept of death. For each lifetime, there is set into motion an appropriate lesson and mission. When that lifetime of learning and achievement has played itself out, it is time to go on to other adventures. Life is an adventure and so is death. At the point of death, you simply walk through a door, a gateway. On the other side indescribable adventures lie in wait. They will, as always, be the most appropriate for your soul's further evolution and joyous journeying back to the Source of your existence.

Understand that I do not suggest you yearn for death. Live in the moment. Live fully in the present, with awareness and maximum attention paid to achieving what you came here for.

I would also like to offer a way for viewing the deaths of those dear to you—a glimpse, as it were, from Spirit's perspective. Those on the other side of the veil have the privilege and honor of welcoming the Beings passing through this transition, returning to the realm of Spirit. A grand welcome home is given those who so valiantly lived the life of Spirit in human or animal form. Spirit salutes those of you who dared to participate in this profound experiment. Death is to be seen as yet another wonder-filled adventure in your continuing trailblazing, homeward bound.

Now Into the Future

Man to the last is but a forward child;
So eager for the future, come what may,
And to the present so insensible!

Samuel Rogers
Reflections

Look! Look over there to the next horizon. Do you see it? Do you see what is in store for you in your future? Wow, isn't it alluring to know that the future may hold wonders (or disasters!) for you and a better (or worse!) life than you now possess?

Now. What are you feeling? Are your shoulders tensed or relaxed? As you look towards your future, consider what your tummy is feeling in this moment. Neck? Eyes? Toes? How are you standing or sitting?

Now. Be here as you read these words. Are you completely being yourSelf? The Self faces the future from the present moment and is actually operating beyond all time in the now. When you come from your present presence, you can act with assuredness as you create your future now.

Pondering prophetic forecasts is tempting, and so I would like to speak about predictions of the future and how to hold them. I suggest that you take them lightly, for predictions are intimately tied to the present feelings, experiences, and concepts of the predictor. Please remember this when you are basing your present day activities on future predictions.

Throughout the ages there have been seers and mystics who, through their gifted natures, have been able to perceive a version of the future. Depending on their abilities, many of these wise ones are able to accurately see what is to be. Yet there are times when the accuracy of even the most gifted prophet has fallen by the wayside. Certain predictions have not come true. Why?

The truth is that predictions are based on the prophet's present day reality, including the prophet's beliefs and experiences. This means many future projections are actually based on the past.

Many of us perceive the present times as special, predicted by prophets of old as the age reaching towards enlightenment. Some of these prophecies have pointed to destruction and earth changes as part of the scenario approaching a new enlightened age. Cleansing and chaos *are* occasionally necessary before true peace can reign. Some of us are fearfully looking forward to more violent earth changes and cata- strophic events. However, there is an alternative view.

We know of the predictions from great seers and prophets such as Edgar Cayce and Nostradamus. We know that some of their more dire predictions have come true in the past. Be aware that there have also been (especially in recent years) many predictions that have not come true. The outcome of the predic- tions were altered. How? By our consciousness. By our progressing enlightenment. By our being in the moment and being with Creator as we create a new future.

It is up to each individual to create his or her own future. Through our consciousness we allow the events and activities to unfold. The visions of seers such as Nostradamus and Cayce were perceived through the eyes of persons living in particular times in history, with all the attitudes and perceptions of those times assisting in the translation of the visions. The futures they saw were predicated upon the fear-based attitudes of their cultures and anticipated continuance of humanity's trend of separation and fear. Some of us have decided to create an alternative to that trend. We are participating in an experimental game called "being here now."

When faced with someone else's information and prophecy about either your individual future or the future of this world, please remember the force of your power as Being. From the present moment you can and will create the future of your choice.

How do you stay in the present moment? It is difficult, to say the least, to completely tame your restless mind in order to achieve that continued presence. First, remember there is no judgment about your mind looking to the past or anticipating the future. But whenever you wish, you can be in the present. How? Just *be here now*. Meditation and disciplines such as t'ai chi or yoga can assist in training all your selves to participate in the now.

As part of your training you can also simply enjoy the ride by asking the Self, "What am I experiencing now?" This is a question that comes in especially handy when you are contemplating prophetic vi-sions. For instance, let's suppose you have had a violent vision of a future that includes death and destruction. Ask your Self in that moment of visioning, "What am I experiencing now?" When you are aware of your experiences in that moment you have the freedom to choose. You may choose to continue your experience as one that is free from fear. You can choose to love where and when and how you are now. That is the key to your future.

Know that our collective souls are creating a golden future. Know that today is eager for your creative touches and flourishes. You might as well have fun with it. You might as well choose to love today. You might as well be here now.

Now, how do you feel?

Forgiveness

Amazing grace, how sweet the sound....
John Newton

The call to be yourSelf boldly is not a call for
perfection. If you are finding that some of the
principles of this book are making you uncomfortable
with the way your life is right now, that's good! The
discomfort will keep you in the game of life, for you
know there is more to learn.   Being yourSelf is a
practice. Sometimes you will experience awareness of
Spirit. Sometimes you will forget you are Spirit. Ah,
how to handle your lack of perfection?

Forgive. Bring the gift of grace into your life.
Forgiveness will cleanse your mind of its many
concerns about attaining the perfect life, for forgiveness does not demand perfection.

As the mother of two little boys, I am often
critical of my parenting skills. I have feared for my
children's lives, I have lied to them, I have raised my
voice in anger. I have alternately loved and hated
being a mom, dipping in and out of the well of
maternal bliss. Though mostly grateful for their
presence, I'm sometimes resentful for the time and
attention they require.

I ask myself, "How can you be a role model for others and speak of such lofty ideals when you're not practicing them in your own life?" And when I've made a particularly large boo-boo, my internal interrogator challenges me, demanding, "What effect are you having on your children? You could be ruining their lives!"

Then the light dawns again. I step out of my dark little box and into the light of Being. I forgive myself. I step back into knowing my freedom of choice and choose to move on.

Many people who attend my lectures and private consultations are initially uncomfortable when they learn of my gift of seeing auras. Knowing full well that I can see their imperfections, they feel ashamed. I can't count the number of times I've heard people say, "My aura must be black."

"Why?" I ask.

"Because I did a terrible thing in my youth." "Because I am addicted to drugs (sex, alcohol, smoking)." "Because I had an abortion." "Because my life is a mess."

What I notice about them is their incredible light. I see their unique ways of reaching for God. I see them doing the best they can.

You are light. In that awareness your forgiving nature will emerge.

You are in a perpetual state of grace. Through forgiveness, the walls of doubt and fear will crumble and fall as you open wide the door to your light-filled Self, leaving the darkness of judgment behind.

Being YourSelf Boldly

By thine own soul's law learn to live,
And if men thwart thee take no heed,
And if men hate thee have no care:
Sing thou thy song and do thy deed.
Hope thou thy hope and pray thy prayer.

Pakenham Beatty
To Thine Own Self Be True

What is the promise of being yourSelf boldly?

It is the promise of life itself. To be boldly
yourSelf means to be living as an eternal manifesta-
tion of God.

When you are being yourSelf boldly you are
operating from the purest of spiritual principles. The
principles of Spirit include all that we have discussed
in this book—awareness, integrity, truth, intuition,
relationship, miracles, and so forth. An interesting
aspect of living by these spiritual principles is that
they do not have any restrictions. They are unbounded and do not operate from judgment. They
are simply the fruits of being wholly who you are.
Moreover, the spiritual principles of being yourSelf
boldly *enhance and ensure your freedom.*

The promise of being yourSelf boldly is the freedom to live your days in the embrace of eternal reality. Present day illusions will come and go. When you are being yourSelf, you recognize illusions for what they are: the imagination of the mind and the constructs of the ego.

Not that the mind and ego are held in judgment. Remember that being yourSelf boldly includes the mind's expressions and offers all aspects of Self a place to be. Even illusions have their day in the sun, and your concepts, beliefs, and opinions have a ballroom in which to wear their costumes and dance.

To be yourSelf boldly is to be in relationship with all. The Being always leaves the door to itSelf open. Being yourSelf boldly is not an exclusive club, it is an inclusive practice that celebrates diversity and unique expression.

The question might have come up, "What exactly do you mean by being bold? Do you mean being assertive or expressive or colorful?" Yes, if that's who you are. And/or quiet, peaceful, composed, and receptive. The key is to express yourSelf, to share the gift of you, and to acknowledge your God-given right and responsibility in Being.

When you operate with boldness there is a spring in your step, a twinkle in your eye and the most exquisite, unending energy flow running through you. As Goethe once said, "Boldness has genius, power and magic in it. Begin it now."

The promise of being yourSelf boldly is the promise of knowing Spirit within you always . . . in all ways.

And Bolder...

I received the following messages after I felt this book had been completed. Two occurred on special anniversaries: On America's Independence Day, 1995, I gained clarity on the possibility of transcending our historical lives via an awakening process (see Emergence). On July 16, the 50th anniversary of the first atomic explosion (code name "Trinity"), came a hopeful and powerful message concerning where the Nuclear Age has brought us. The final chapter illuminates the timeless phenomenon known as inspiration, revealing its purpose and equal accessibility to all of humankind. All three transmissions are powerful messages for our human society and were assisted by a group energy who called itself the "Lighted Ones." I liked the name, and as I worked with this energy, I felt surrounded by loving, compassionate Life.

Emergence

From of old there are not lacking things that have attained
*   Oneness.*
The sky attained Oneness and became clear;
The earth attained Oneness and became calm;
The spirits attained Oneness and became charged with
*   mystical powers;*
The fountains attained Oneness and became full;
The ten thousand creatures attained oneness and became
*   reproductive;*
Barons and princes attained Oneness and became
*   sovereign rulers of the world.*
All of them are what they are by virtue of Oneness.

Lao Tzu
Tao Teh Ching
translated by John C.H. Wu

Psst. You there. You know who you are. The Angel in
hiding. Won't you come out and play today? Won't you
come out and shine your light so at least one other being
will feel the warmth of Creator's love?

This is a message to an awakening humanity.
Awakening is a process that can be gentle or dramatic, your choice. What you are waking up to are

new dimensions of your soul and new layers of consciousness. You can journey to these states of awareness without ever moving through time or space. Awakening happens right where you are and when you are being.

Just the fact that you are participating in this experiment called "Spirit in Matter" gives you the opportunity to become a fully awakened master. A fully awakened master knows there is no separation between what was, what is, and what will be. The master also knows there is no separation between you and me, male and female, Arab and Jew, American and African, European and Asian. No separation exists between the animal kingdom and the mineral kingdom and the kingdom of the plants and the human kingdom. All is united in Creation. *All is*. If you see the magnificence of this truth, you are an awakened master. It is that simple. There is really nothing to it. This is waking up.

You might perceive awakening as a process to be undergone. Because of this perception we offer you a bit of perspective: As you awaken to the fact of your divine essence, you might find you are a bit groggy at first. It is as if you have been asleep for a long while and, after you awaken, you find you have to take time to rub the sleep sand from your eyes. In your spiritual awakening you will also take time to rub the sands of history from your human eyes. In order to see clearly, pay attention to your body's feelings as it awakens with you.

Your cells have been locked into a historical structure that is no longer functioning well. You will have to retrain the body to become a spiritually aware body. You do this by paying attention to the body's callings and urgent pleas.

The body will show signs of cellular restructuring
that include feelings of light-headedness, dizziness,
electrical impulse, whirling sensations starting from
the ground up, ringing in the ears, congestion in the
throat and the bronchial area, pain or discomfort in
the shoulders, a fullness or buzzing in what is known
as the third eye. These are some of the symptoms
your body will give in acknowledgment of its
attunement to the awakening process.

In order for you to assist the awakening body, you
might want to consider doing the following:

1. Massage and deep-tissue body work are essential for the cell's release of their historical remem-
brances. Make certain the person touching your body
is of the highest integrity.

2. Flower and crystal essences and plant aromas
attune your body to the color and rhythm of nature.
Realize that nature, in the form of Mother Earth, is
also awakening to her divinity.

3. Connect with Creator every day. Still meditation is best. Relaxation and movement are good also,
provided you are consciously aligning yourSelf with
Source.

4. Pay attention to the energy of people who
surround you—including your acquaintances, family
members, and work colleagues. Be aware that you
might have some "farewelling" to do with those who
no longer serve in your evolution and who have
already received the maximum benefit of your
presence. This might sound like a cruel recommendation; but we suggest it is also cruel to hang onto
energies that no longer serve. Make these separations
with love, and send these loved ones on their particular and special journeys with the greatest of respect.

5. Be vigilant. Notice when you are feeling off-centered. It is at these times you may be prone to accepting vibrations into your energy field that will not benefit you. In other words, when you are feeling unbalanced, the forces of forgetfulness (a.k.a. the dark forces) are more prone to influence you. Be vigilant, and ask especially of the disembodied entities you encounter if they are of the Light. We ask you to pay attention to how you feel about their answer. Next, if you feel that any communication from these beings carries even a hint of judgment, send these beings on their way. They will not serve you if they are here to judge you.

Awakening is essentially a process of lightening up. Given your permission, your body, emotions, mind, and soul will unite to easily travel through inter-dimensional gateways to the Halls of Remembrance.

We wish to gently caution you as to your mind's racing ahead, trying to figure out when and how this is going to happen. Our answer, dear Sisters and Brothers, is *you are awakening now.* It is in the Halls of Remembrance within your own Being that you will recognize your Self, your place in the universe, and the others that shine along with you. Do not fear or be anxious. Go forth and know that you are exactly and precisely where you need to be in the process. We, the Lighted Ones, salute you and encourage you and will continue to encourage the Awakening Ones. We are watching you grow and, with patience and awe, we are awaiting your return to full consciousness.

From the Nuclear Age
to the Age of Miracles

*One touch of nature makes the
whole world kin . . .*

William Shakespeare
Troilus and Cressida

**What was the reason for the Nuclear Age and
where are we heading?**

The Nuclear Age was allowed to happen by
Creator and those Lighted Ones who, in their love for
humanity, wished to test the limits of the dance with
matter at the absolute edge of forgetfulness. Using
atomic energy and unleashing a destructive force that
holds within it the keys to the secrets of creation was
and is an experiment in knowing how far forgetfulness will take a race.

We Lighted Ones wish you no harm. We only
wish for you to reach out of your boundaries of
separation from the rest of us. This play, "The Nuclear
Age," is a drama. The plot began when you uncov-
ered a particular mystery that can be used for destruc-

tion or creation. This drama involves the use of knowledge disconnected from Spirit, and that is why we call it a lesson in forgetfulness—the ultimate lesson in forgetfulness.

We who daily play with and understand the so-called secrets of the universe know that the partnership with our colleagues, the atomic and subatomic particles, is not an evil thing. We who are constantly connected with all that is know the atomic connection is eternally entwined within Creator. We do not have the illusion that we are operating alone. We know that all play in the universe is divinely guided, including this experiment on your planet called the use and abuse of free will. It was in divine love that you were given the opportunity and the *choice* of using your personal and group will to decide which path to take as you evolve. Evolution itself warranted a necessary testing of the limits of your willfulness.

When your race began to see beyond the illusion of three-dimensional reality and became acquainted with your co-inhabitants in the small (atomic) world, you were playing at a very basic level of creation and, depending on the consciousness of your race, could have used this knowledge to bring you closer to Creator's lap. Instead, much like your teenagers and your two-year-old children, you have decided to run away from the lap of God and use this new creative power to extend and push your will to see how far it will go.

We observe that now, in this present age of reckoning, you are becoming mature people, closer to acknowledging and utilizing the wisdom of your Being. It is time for humanity to approach adulthood, and we Lighted Ones are now communicating in force—in droves, in crowds—so that many of you will recognize opportunities to gain knowledge of the creative interaction between Spirit and will. True maturity will occur in this age which we call the "Age of Miracles."

Out of the Age of Miracles will evolve a partnership between human will, the individual personality, and the love of Spirit. This consortium (or trinity) of will, personality, and Spirit will take humanity beyond the dangers of utilizing atomic power in ignorance. We have witnessed the destruction of many planets and planetary systems that have taken this road. The Age of Miracles will emphasize spiritual input and assistance in all human expressions.

Know that whatever actions you take here on Earth are felt in a ripple effect by many other planetary and starlike entities throughout the universe. It is as though your planet were a place on a web, and when this planet moves a certain way, the rest of the web feels the effect of its movement. The explosive movement that occurred in July of 1945 was felt by many concerned and awed Beings throughout your galaxy. Those of us most concerned about the outcomes of this "experiment of will" have gathered forces to assist you in knowing there is another way to use the knowledge you have gained via the discovery of atomic force in your lives. You will incorporate your remembrance of the Love Force, or Spirit, in willing your evolutionary path. You will be *responsibly* responsible in the creation of your destiny. The Age of Miracles is an age of miracles created by you.

Technology without Spirit is a path to death. You can see some effects of this technology without Spirit on the Internet. Without love as the driver, the use of communication technology will only lead to dead ends—dead ends in meaningful relationship and dead ends in constructive communication. We are not critiquing the Internet, just illuminating the more extreme levels of forgetfulness it sometimes promotes (i.e., excessive materialism and cyberpornography).

Technology is a man-made construct; however, Spirit breathed life into Man, and so technology can be driven by Spirit as well. You will know the Dawn of the Age of Miracles when you respond less to the phenomena of technology and more to your spiritual drive. You will then use technology to the fullest advantage for all.

We wish to remind you of Nature's role in this era of technological wonders and nuclear experimentation. The atomic and subatomic particles are the elemental bases for all of Nature. It is Nature who has allowed herself to be tapped and probed for the means and ways to project your will as far as it will go. Now is the time to remember her in all her generous forms as she participates in your lives. She is the role model for how to evolve in matter and Spirit. Look to Nature's patterns to learn how to proceed in your experimental projects, especially those you call high-tech.

Nature provides a model of balance and rootedness that many of you have forgotten. Remember, the inventions that have propelled you into the era of technological progress have resulted through the observation of Nature—hence your airplanes and helicopters,even your temperamental toasters. Welcome Nature back into your technological lives. Listen, pay attention to her calls and threats. There are limits to how much of her energy she will allow to be used without Spirit as the driving force. Spirit will gladly assume a larger role in your evolutionary growth, drawing you closer to the Love Force that is, after all, the original Creator of Nature, your free will, and your technology.

We wish to make a recommendation: Do not despair! Because you have stretched your will to its maximum boundary line, you have experienced what it is like to progress scientifically and technologically based solely on your community's will. We ask you not to despair because we are noting the subtle yet powerful voice of Spirit being heard throughout the lands. This voice grows ever stronger as it enters and influences the thoughts of those who are involved in technological wonders and experimentation with atomic and subatomic energy.

Those of us called the Lighted Ones will assist you to incorporate the will of Spirit into the very fabric of your technological advances. We will recommend observation of and respect for the natural world. Look to nature for ideas in the cleansing process of this polluted and corrupted planet. Nature holds the key to the destructive force; She holds the key to the creative force as well. Do not despair. Get to work. Love what you are and even how you have been in the past. The Love Force will lift you out of despair and outrage and fear into a higher knowing that nothing, *no-thing* is ever destroyed! Your destructive toys do not reek the eternal havoc you think they do.

The Love Force of Creator will prevail and you, the stars of "Operation Planet of Miracles" will bring the light of this force into the homes, laboratories, schools, halls of justice, marketplace, and places of political play. We know how much you have wanted reassurance. Our reassurance comes in the form of an observation: Other planets have adjusted, via the road of forgetfulness and willfulness, to the central road of the Love Force interacting with matter.

Having witnessed this many times over, we know Love will prevail. This is not only a call to faith, this can be known at the core of your Being.

Stepping from the Nuclear Age into the Age of Miracles is easy because you *are* the Age of Miracles. You are the champions of Love. And for this we bless you and acknowledge the wonder of you.

Inspiration

Inside, outside, below, above . . .
See your light and feel its love.
You're asking you when you ask me,
So you know everything, don't you see?

Chara M. Curtis
All I See is Part of Me

Tell us about inspiration.

Inspiration comes when the mind is clear and the boundaries of the ego are lowered. It comes the instant you need it, breaking through the surface of unconsciousness. In that moment, the universe is your oyster and the world your pearl. Inspiration is an event, a feeling and a divine right for all human beings.

For many eons, humanity has been toiling under the yoke of forgetfulness and fear. Very difficult taskmasters, these, for they ask you to keep plowing and planting their dark seeds. Inspiration was invented to break through the walls of fearful thinking and bring you momentary peace.

Inspirational writing, music, and art have kept the human race interested in wanting to continue. Without inspiration this race would have expired many eons ago. Through the inspirational energy of Spirit coming through the voice of people willing to listen, a trail of hope has been carved out for humanity to walk along . . . back into the Light, back into Creator's warmth. From the coldest, most dismal times of this planet came some of the most inspirational leaders. Out of war and separation and the grief of entire nations, certain persons stilled and cleared themselves enough to hear Spirit's inspiration calling them home, with the entreaty to call the rest of humanity home as well. Isis, Lao Tsu, Jesus, Mary, Buddha, Mohammed, Chief Sealth, Gandhi, Martin Luther King, Gorbachev, Beethoven, Mozart, John Lennon, Michelangelo, Van Gogh, Miro, Thoreau, Joseph Campbell, Deepak Chopra, Maya Angelou, the Dalai Lama—these are but a few examples of people who heard the voice within them and chose to listen and act.

How are you inspired in your life? Do you pause to bring inspiration to your every day, or do you just get through the day somehow? Usually, inspiration comes in a moment of quiet or desperation. It is also possible for inspiration to come through people when they are simply ready for something new, fresh, and more deeply satisfying than the yammering and stammering and monotonous droning of mass culture's voice. The inspiring people of today listen impeccably to the voice of Spirit and then *move*.

Inspirational writing and art challenge you to look within and rediscover your heart. They inspire you to get off the couch and into the streets of humanity, where you can spread your light doing what needs to get done. Inspirational teachings are here to make you ponder what life is all about. They pose more questions and challenges than they answer. In this way they support your freedom of thought and knowing.

You can only know who you are by being absolutely meticulous in your life of service. "Meticulous" means you are in integrity with your Spiritual calling. You are meant to be a whole and holy human being. Human. Being. The integration of these two elements of creation is what you are here to immerse yourSelf in. Being complete. Being holy. Being yourSelf.

To be completely in integrity with Spirit's inspirations requires that you not become immersed in the cultural mayhem and prevalent disjointed thinking that promotes forgetfulness and separation. This means you might want to make some lifestyle changes that would, perhaps, include the following:

1. Turn off the TV. If you cannot do that yet, at least turn off news programs. These little bits of images and sound infiltrate and permeate your psyche and promote more fear than should actually exist in your system. If you are so inclined, you may wish to occasionally pick up a newspaper or tune into the radio to keep current with the local and world situation. Even so, these forms of media also tend to promote drama and fearful thinking, so use discernment and caution.

2. Keep your words of alarm, drama, crisis, and hopelessness to a minimum when you are chatting with others. There is a particular club you might wish to avoid altogether: the Ain't-It-Awful Club. The Ain't-It-Awful Club is designed to keep you "in the pits." It disrupts your creative force to commiserate

and muck around with those who proclaim their lives to be terrible. Do not subscribe to this club.

Answer the question "How are you?" truthfully. No matter how you respond, end your answer on a positive note. For instance, if you are feeling physically ill and someone asks how you are, you might answer, "My body is ill at this time. It is undergoing a cleansing process and I appreciate my body as it is doing so." Telling the truth to another and seeing the light in another will disassemble the ain't-it-awful thoughts more quickly than the blink of an eye.

3. Acknowledge at least three other beings each day. Approach three other beings—be they plant, mineral, animal, or human—and acknowledge them for their existence in and contribution to your life. Consider all in your life to be mirrors for you. Your gifts of warm compliments and acknowledgment gift you as well. You enter into a grateful state of mind, another doorway to inspiration.

In order for you to be inspired and inspiring, you need to know that you have something to share with the world. Many of you feel you do not have much to offer in the way of inspiration. That simply is not true. You can inspire another with your smile, with your positive outlook, or with your compassion. These are examples of inspirational acts. You do have it within you to inspire.

For those of you who have had a difficult time knowing that *Be YourSelf Boldly* is an inspired work, please note that inspirational communications are created with those on the other side of forgetfulness as a message of hope to your awakening humanity. The *Be YourSelf Boldly* inspirations are no different. Spirit is connected with you. Spirit loves you dearly. I offer these inspired lessons out of my sincere intention to communicate from Spirit, hopeful that you, too, have chosen to acknowledge and utilize your Spirit connection.

Opening your heart to your own inspirations is a lovely prelude to a life of wonder. You will feel truly alive when you listen to your heart's song. Sing loudly and boldly for all to hear your inspiring voice.

Spirit dances to the tune of Its own voice.

A Blessing

Returning to mySelf
I sit by the Sea of Life itself
And look into the crystal waters.
A voice calls my name.
Its location is in the Sea before me.
It is calling for me to be mySelf.

I answer that I am very present;
That I have returned to the sea to be mySelf
Boldly.
The voice replies,
"You are mySelf.
You are the voice in the sea,
You are the Sea of Life itSelf."

Gently I turn to the future. I face it with renewed
vigor,
For I know of it.
It is my creation;
In my Being I have conceived it;
Its birth is in my hands.
I rejoice and be mySelf.
It is in that Boldness that the grace and ease
of living my life makes itself known.

I feel blessed.
And that I am.

Bob Branscom
Dedicated to the memory
and the presence of his Being.